INDIANS

The First Americans

By PATRICIA MILES MARTIN

Illustrated by ROBERT FRANKENBERG

Published by
FIREFLY PAPERBACKS
A Scholastic Book Service

To Cherokee Smith

3 4 5 6 7 8 9 0 - 8 7 6 5 4 3 2 1 0

Printed in U.S.A.

ISBN 0-590-38005-2

CONTENTS

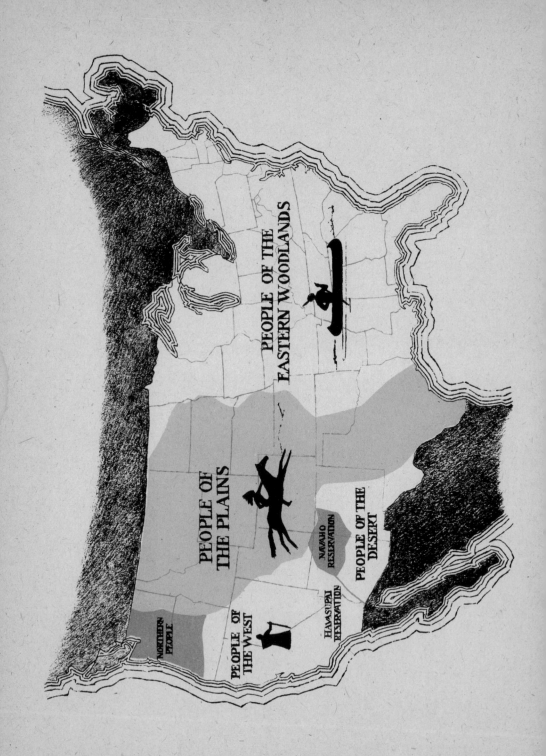

PEOPLE OF THE
EASTERN WOODLANDS

PEOPLE OF
THE PLAINS

PEOPLE OF THE DESERT

NAVAHO RESERVATION

HAVASUPAI RESERVATION

PEOPLE OF
THE WEST

NORTHERN PEOPLE

Chapter I
THE FIRST AMERICANS

The Indians were the first Americans.

They did not call themselves Indians. They called themselves The People.

Hundreds of years ago, before white colonists came to settle on the land and to build their homes, The People lived in America. Many tribes were in the woodlands, on the grasslands, on the deserts, and in the forests.

Each man was loyal to his tribe. Each was loyal to his family. Each shared his food with those who had no food, and shared his shelter with those who had no shelter.

In this long ago time, no tribe had a written language. Each tribe spoke a language different from that of any other tribe. But each separate tribe remembered its own stories that had been told by the old to the young for hundreds of years.

Some of the stories were about their history. Some were about the fox and the snake, the bear and the eagle. The People told their stories in songs and in dances.

Often they sang and danced for the pleasure it gave them. Sometimes they sang and danced their prayers to the Great Spirit that watched over all men and wild things, over trees and rocks, rivers and earth. Often The People danced a prayer to the Rain God, asking for rain. When the good rain came, they danced their prayer of thanks to the Rain God for the rain that had been given them.

The People went to their Medicine Man when they were sick. And with his magic and mystery, the Medicine Man cared for them.

Sometimes he chanted and sang secret words that only the Indians knew. Sometimes he gave them herbs and roots that made them well.

Many tribes were warlike. With bows and arrows and clubs, they raided other tribes and took what they wanted. But some tribes were peaceful and traded with one another. And those people who traded in peace learned from each other. They learned how to weave, how to plant, how to care for sheep. They learned about tribal dances.

Chapter II
THE PEOPLE OF
THE WOODLANDS

When the white men first came to America, there were many tribes in the woodlands of the East. There in the woodlands, where the land was fertile, The People used what the land gave them.

The men hunted in the woods for deer. They knew how to take the sap from the maple tree to make syrup. They trapped the beaver and caught the wild turkey. They fished in the clear rivers.

The People lived in villages. Their longhouses were covered with bark. Often they built strong

stockades of long poles fixed in the ground and set close together, to make their villages safe from warring tribes. A few tribes in the woodlands lived in tepees. They made a tepee of straight poles, in the shape of a great cone, and covered it over with bark.

In the winter, the men wore shirts and skirts made of buckskin from the hide of the deer they had killed. They wore soft buckskin moccasins. The women wore skirts they had

woven from the wild grasses. They wrapped
themselves in warm furs.

In the summer, the women wore their grass-
woven skirts and the men wore breechcloths.
The children wore nothing at all.

At home, the girls helped care for the small
fields near their villages—fields of beans and
squash and corn. They ground the corn to make
their bread.

The boys went with their fathers to hunt.
Softly, they crept through the woods with bows
and arrows and clubs. Silently, they guided their
birchbark canoes down the rivers.

When the hunt was over, the deer gave them meat to eat and buckskin for clothes and for moccasins.

If the men were skillful, they made beads from shells. Only a careful workman could shape the brittle shell into a long slim piece, and drill the long hole to make a bead. They made many beads and strung them on slim pieces of rawhide. The beads told the story of their tribe.

When the settlers first came, friendly woodland Indians showed them how to plant corn and beans, how to follow the Indian trails to hunt the deer.

Chapter III
THE PEOPLE OF THE DESERT

At the time the settlers came to the woodlands, there were also many tribes on the desert. Some tribes lived in houses of earth that dotted the desert.

Some tribes of the desert lived in villages high on a bluff above a river. They lived in stone houses, with steep trails that led down to the river.

Below, by the river, they grew their squash and corn, beans and melons.

If raiders tried to climb the rocky trail, those in the village rolled rocks down against their enemies. And The People were safe on their high bluff as long as there was corn in their baskets and water in their jars.

Some of The People lived in houses of sun-baked bricks and stone, in a village high on the flat land. Many men of the tribes were skillful workmen. They made belts and necklaces of silver and turquoise. The women wove baskets from the wild grasses that grew on the desert.

In the desert, Indians harvested the red fruit of the cactus. From the fruit, they made jam for sweet food. They made wine to use in their tribal rites when they asked the Rain God to send a gift of rain.

In a canyon on the desert The People raised their corn. It was beautiful corn with red, blue, yellow, and black kernels on each ear.

Chapter IV

THE PEOPLE OF THE PLAINS

When the white settlers arrived in the woodlands, many tribes met on the plains. They followed the buffalo herd. When he went to hunt, the hunter took his tepee with him. Two long poles were fastened against a horse's shoulders. The ends of the poles dragged on the ground, and the tepee was lashed to the ends of the poles.

The hunter was ready to ride away.

When the wandering tribes met on the plains, they set up their tepees in a circle and tethered their horses near their tepees.

Though one tribe did not know the other's language, all tribes of the plains learned a sign language, and they talked with each other, using their signs.

There, in the circle of tepees, they held their rites to call the buffalo.

In their rites, they told the story of a great flood, of a big canoe tossing on the waters.

They told of a man in the canoe, who sent a white dove to bring back a green leaf to tell him that land was near.

In their rites, they danced to the beating of drums.

Often they sent messages over a long distance, with smoke signals. They built a smoky fire. Two men held a blanket over the fire. Flipping the blanket away from the fire and back again, they sent out small puffs of smoke that were seen from far away.

Sometimes they sent their messages by the beating of their drums.

When the message came that the buffalo herd was in sight, the men leaped on their horses and galloped away.

The buffalo gave the hunters many things The People needed. There was buffalo meat to eat, fur for clothing and for tepees, horns for spoons, ropes to be made from strips of rawhide, and bones to be made into tools.

The Indian girls helped prepare the buffalo hide. From the hide, the women made beautiful clothing.

Warfare was common on the plains. Often a few Indians rode away to raid another tribe. Quickly they would strike, take what they wanted—horses, slaves—and quickly ride away.

Proudly, the warriors of the plains wore the eagle feather and the tall war bonnet with its long banner of feathers.

Chapter V

THE PEOPLE OF THE WEST

When the settlers first came to the woodlands, there were many Indian tribes in the West, between the plains and the sea. Each tribe used what the land gave them.

Along the warm coast, the seed gatherers roamed through their pleasant land, finding their food as it ripened—acorns, nuts, berries. They fished in the rivers and found clams on the beaches. In this warm land, they needed little clothing.

In the redwood forests of the North were the hunters and the fishermen.

With bows and arrows and spears, they hunted the antelope and the deer and the mountain goat. With nets and traps, they fished in the rivers. In huge dug-out canoes made from great trees, they hunted the whale in the ocean.

They made their strong houses with slabs from the cedar tree. They carved tall poles to stand in front of their strong wooden houses. Much as ranchers today burn their brands on their cattle and on their gates, so the Indians carved their own signs on the tops of their totem poles. Below the signs, they carved the story of their pride in their people.

From the cedar tree, they carved bowls and spoons.

They carved mysterious masks to use in their tribal rites.

The women wove blankets from cedar bark and the hair of the mountain goat, to keep the family warm in winter. And they wove cone-shaped basket hats from reeds and grasses to protect themselves from the rain.

In the summer, the women wore their skirts of cedar bark.

When the men went out to raid another tribe, they wore helmets carved of wood, and carried their wooden clubs and bows and arrows.

Far up north, where the winters were
long and cold, The People were hunters.

On foot, they wandered far to hunt the
moose, the beaver, and the elk. They hunted
with bows and arrows and clubs. They caught fish
with spears and snares. When they could
not find enough wild game for their food, they
dug in the earth and found roots to eat.

Some lived in shelters that were dug under-
ground. Some lived in tepees covered with
brush or with skins of animals they had killed.

These people were often hungry. They sang
their tribal stories about their starving people.

Chapter VI
THE PEOPLE AND THE LAND

Wherever they were—in the woodlands or on the plains, in the forests or on the desert— The People took what the land gave them, and they were thankful to the earth and the sun and the rain.

In all tribes, The People respected the things of nature—buffalo and deer, squirrel and rabbit. They did not kill a wild creature for the pleasure of the hunt. They killed to get food. They killed to live.

They respected the rocks and the trees and the green things that grew from the earth. Often the Indian prayed to the Great Spirit, "May I know the lessons you have hidden under every leaf . . ."

Chapter VII
THE RESERVATIONS

When the colonists came to North America, they built their homes where the Indians lived and hunted. Sometimes the white men offered to buy the land where the Indians lived, but the Indians believed that the land belonged to all people. Like the air around them, like the sun and moon in the sky, the land was not something to sell.

The white settlers had come to stay.
Sometimes they tricked the Indians into selling
the land. When the Indians understood what
had been done, they fought to keep their land.

Indians killed settlers and their families and
burned their cabins. Settlers killed Indians and
burned their villages. And so, wrong piled upon
wrong. The Indians could not win against the
white man's guns.

The United States Government wanted peace
for the settlers. It decided to move all Indians

to reservations—land set aside for their use.

The Government made treaties with many tribes. In the treaties, the Government made its promises. It promised to set aside land for the tribes. The Indians were to keep the land forever. "As long as the grass shall grow and the rivers run," were the words in a treaty.

The Government promised to give the Indians seeds for their first planting. It promised to start schools for Indian children.

The Indians signed the treaties. They promised they would not fight. They would obey the laws of the United States.

But treaties were broken.

Sometimes the treaties were broken by the Indians. They did not understand that they had promised to leave their homelands. Sometimes the Chief who signed a treaty did not have the right to sign for all of his tribe.

Treaties were broken again and again by white men who took the good land that had been given to the Indians. The settlers built their homes on Indian land.

Tribe by tribe, almost all Indians were forced to leave the woodlands and go to land that the settlers did not want for their own use.

A few Indian families had left their reservations to live among the settlers. These families stayed on, in the East.

Five tribes had taken the ways of the white man. They had lived in peace. They obeyed the laws of the United States. They farmed their good land and they made their own tribal laws. They had schools for their children, they dressed as the white man dressed. But the settlers wanted their land, and these five tribes were also moved on to the West.

A few woodland Indians were allowed to stay on small reservations in the East, but most

Indians were forced to go to reservations west of the Mississippi River. Some tribes in the West were given a small part of their own homelands to use.

The Indians had lived for hundreds of years in America. All tribes loved the earth and were thankful for the life it gave them. When they left their homelands to go to the reservations, they left the land as they had found it. The trees still grew tall and thick in the forests.

The waters of the rivers ran cold and clear.
The beauty of the land was not changed.

On the reservations, the Indians planted the
seeds that had been given them. But there was
not enough food for their people. Many Indians
died. The Government ordered food to be sent
to the starving people, but too often it arrived
spoiled and unfit to eat.

A few Government schools were started for
the children. White people from outside, who
cared about the children, also started schools on
the reservations.

On big reservations, there was no school for most children, because their families lived so far apart that not enough children could walk to the same school.

Often Indian fathers did not want their children to learn the ways of the white man.

So, for many years, most girls and boys did not go to school.

Today, there are schools for all children. There are day schools and boarding schools. For the boys and girls on the big reservations who live too far away to go to school, sometimes the school is sent to them in a trailer.

Chapter VIII

THE HAVASUPAI

One of the smallest tribes in the United States today is that of the Havasupai, The People of the Blue-green Water.

At the bottom of Havasu canyon, walled around by red-brown sandstone cliffs, is the Havasupai reservation. The reservation was the homeland of the first Havasupai. These friendly people have lived here for hundreds of years.

The reservation lies within the area of the

Grand Canyon National Park in Arizona, but it is not a part of the park.

Down in the deep canyon, beyond the little village of Supai, are the tumbling, churning, blue-green waters of Havasu Falls.

The Havasupai must obey the laws of the United States. Also, they obey their own tribal laws.

These people of the Blue-green Water elect a tribal council. The men and women who are elected make the laws for the good of their tribe.

There are three Chiefs on the reservation. One of the Chiefs is a Deputy Sheriff. He is the policeman for his tribe.

Some of The People live in round-roofed houses built of mud and brush. Some live in two-room houses made of boards. There are houses of red sandstone, and there are small stone cottages.

The men of the tribe wear jeans and bright shirts, big hats and cowboy boots. And the dress of the Indian women is like that worn by the women on a western ranch. Boys and girls on the reservation wear clothes like those worn by all boys and girls outside the reservation.

Little fields are planted near the houses, and peach trees grow in the orchards.

There in the canyon, The People still plant their Indian corn with red, white, yellow, blue, and black kernels on the same ear. They plant it exactly as their forefathers did, hundreds of years ago.

Corn grows high, and peach trees bear their fine harvest of fruit, here where there is water for men to use.

The People of the Blue-green Water grow squash and beans and melons.

Other food is packed down the long trail from the town above. Many horses and mules carry sugar and coffee, bacon and flour, potatoes and soda pop down the long trail.

Both men and women work to be able to buy the food that is brought in.

Once there was a school on the reservation. White teachers came and white teachers left, for they found it lonely at the bottom of the canyon.

When the Government passed a law that all children should go to boarding schools on the outside, the old schoolhouse was closed. For many years it has been empty, its bell silent.

All children from seven to sixteen years of age are taken outside to a boarding school for Indian children. Up the trail they go, children and mothers and fathers. On burro, on mule, or by horseback, they ride to meet the bus that will take the children far away to school.

When the boys and girls leave, they know they will not see their canyon until the next vacation. It is an unhappy day when the bus takes the youngest children away for the first time.

In the summer, laughing girls and boys ride

their horses, or splash in the cold water of the creek.

If one of The People on the reservation must be taken to a hospital, an Air Force helicopter settles down in the canyon and takes its passenger to a hospital outside.

Many non-Indians come from outside to see the reservation. Some of the Indian men are guides who take the visitors far down the canyon. The Indian women make baskets to sell to the visitors. The visitors also hire the Indians' horses and buy the harvest of peaches.

When the peaches are ripe, The People have a Peach Festival. At the festival, they have a rodeo, with bucking horses and calf roping. Afterward, the men and women and children dance their tribal dances and sing their stories.

Often, Navaho men come from their reservation to ride in the rodeo.

Chapter IX

THE NAVAHOS

The Navaho reservation is the largest reservation in the United States.

This is the Indian Country that the Navahos love. It is sandy, flat land, with deep mysterious canyons.

The reservation is in Arizona and New Mexico, and reaches north into the state of Utah. It is a part of land that was once their homeland. It is a vast land, this land of the Navaho.

Some of the Navahos live on a small part of the reservation where there is water for their fields. But most of The People live on the beautiful red-brown flat land of the desert, where water is scarce.

There are towns on the reservation—towns with small buildings and neat two-room houses and shacks covered with tar paper. Most of The People do not live in the towns.

Once the Navahos were a warlike people who took what they wanted from their neighbors.

Now they drive their small flocks of sheep over the hot desert. They find little streams where their sheep may drink. They find small green patches of grass growing in the shade of the red rock cliffs.

Most of the Navahos live in hogans which are scattered over their desert. The hogans are usually built with six or eight sides. Each hogan has a small door and a smoke hole in the top of the rounded roof.

When it is time to eat, the woman builds a low fire in the center of the hogan, and there she cooks the food for her family. Sometimes they have meat to eat. More often, they have beans and squash and fried bread.

Almost every family has its horse. Dogs run everywhere.

The women wear long, bright skirts and velvet blouses. The men wear jeans and the big hat of the western cowboy, but they wear soft boots made of buckskin. The Navaho children dress as non-Indian children dress outside the reservation.

If a Navaho is sick, his family drives him to a hospital. If his family does not have a car, a neighbor will be glad to lend his.

On the reservation, little yellow buildings with three sides, roofed over against the hot sun, mark the places where the bus stops to pick up girls and boys who are going to Government school.

The reservation is large and the hogans are far apart. Sometimes a boy or a girl has to walk a long, long way from his hogan to the bus station. The bus may go many miles to the nearest school.

Children are also taught by their mothers

and fathers. The child shares in the work to be done. He has his part in the rites of his tribe. His teaching is carefully planned. Each child becomes a good member of his tribe.

"Speak softly," the Navaho mother says. "Speak the truth."

"Do not be afraid," the Navaho father says. "Be brave."

Indian fathers and mothers do not scold their children, for they believe that it is not good to speak harsh words to a child.

When Navaho boys and girls first go to school today, many must learn a second language—English. The child in school must not only learn to read and write, to spell and to count, but he must learn many things that are new to him. He must learn that on the outside the land does not belong to all people. He must learn about money and how to count it.

The Navahos on the reservation must obey

the laws of the United States. They must also obey their own tribal laws.

Some time ago, oil was discovered on the reservation. Most of the money the Navahos receive from the sale of the oil is carefully spent by the Navaho Tribal Council for the good of all its people. With some of the money, it sends young Navahos to universities.

The Navahos are eager to help themselves.

Life on the reservation is harsh for most of The People, for the corn does not grow where water is scarce. The Navaho works in the fields. He tends his sheep. But he must find other work, if he is to buy food for his family. Too often, the Navaho cannot find work on the reservations.

Some Navahos are silver workers.

In his hogan, the Navaho makes necklaces and belts, setting the blue turquoise stones in silver, as his forefathers did.

Many women make beautiful baskets from grasses found in the desert. Almost every woman weaves rugs that are sold at the Trading Post.

Outside the hogan, she sits in front of her loom, weaving her pattern into the rug, day after day after day.

The families that live in the hogans must carry the water they use. They often carry water from long distances. Water is too scarce to be used for washing dishes. The mother and the girls of the family scrub their dishes with sand. Water is only to drink, and to dribble over each plant in the field to help it grow.

When they need water, the whole family—grandmother, mother, father, children—hitch a horse to an old spring wagon. They load the wagon with their empty cans and jars. From the oldest to the youngest, they climb into the wagon and off they go. Perhaps they know where a spring bubbles from the earth. Perhaps

they drive to the nearest filling station where they fill their cans and jars from the water tap.

Only a few families have running water in their houses. They are the families who live in small Government-built houses in the little towns. Perhaps the father is a Navaho Ranger. In his old car, he rides to work in the pine forest in a corner of the reservation. Perhaps he is a Navaho policeman. Perhaps he works in the filling station or at the Trading Post.

In the Trading Post, food and clothes and

tools are sold or traded. The Trading Post is also a bank. It is a post office. It is a place where Navahos meet and visit with each other.

The Navahos are a friendly people. Often they meet to dance their tribal dances and sing their tribal songs.

Their Medicine Man has kept in his memory

all the old songs and chants of the Navaho, and he knows how to make the dry paintings that are used in their rites. He grinds colored rocks until they become a fine powder. He works with small piles of blue and white, yellow and black powder. He lets the colored powder flow from his fingertips, as he makes a dry painting on the ground. To the Navaho, the dry painting is like the altar of a church.

At harvest time, people of many tribes go to the Navaho Tribal Fair, with its rodeo and grand parade. The old-time Navaho is there with his long hair, the young Navaho with his hair cut short.

Here at the Fair, they show the things they have grown, the finest of their corn and squash. They show the beautiful blankets and baskets they have made and the sheep they have raised.

The Navaho takes from the red-brown land that which the land has to give him—green patches of grass for his sheep, earth for his pottery, grasses for his baskets, squash and beans and corn for his food.

Chapter X

INDIANS IN THE CITIES

Today, on most reservations, the Indians dress much the same as the non-Indian does. Many older people do not speak English. Their younger children do not speak English unless they have learned to speak it in school.

Long ago, the Indians had to live in Indian Country. Years later, when they were hungry on the reservations, the Government urged them to work and live outside.

Some Indians have left their reservations

because they believe that their children must have an education to find a better way to live.

Some have left because they were soldiers in the United States Army. They saw the outside, and liked the things they saw.

If an Indian decides that he will take his family to live in the city, the United States Government will send him to the city. He will be trained to become a barber, a cook, a watchmaker, a shoemaker . . .

In many cities, the Indian will find a meeting place—an Indian Center—where he can find friendship. In the Indian Centers all tribes are welcome. In their powwows, all tribes dance the same dances, whether they come from the desert or the mountains, the plains or the woodlands. In many Indian Centers, all tribes wear the dress of the Plains Indian with his eagle feather and his war bonnet.

In the Indian Center, the Indian who is new to the city will find help.

But the ways of the people in the city are strange to the Indian from the reservation.

Maybe the Indian comes from a place where time is measured by the sun and by the harvest of corn. Maybe he comes from the quiet lands. He finds in the noisy city great buildings rising as high as his hills. He has a new and strange trail to follow. He finds it hard to learn the ways of people outside. He is bewildered and he is proud.

If he finds work that he can do, he has yet to learn that when a man works in the city, he must work every day, and at the same hours. He must learn many new ways.

When he earns money, he buys his first

television set. Often the money that he earns
is quickly gone, for if a friend is hungry,
he gives him food. If a friend needs shelter,
he gives him shelter.

Many Indians go back to Indian Country.
If he decides to go back, the Indian knows that
his life will be hard on the reservation. He
may be hungry. But perhaps trying to learn
new ways in a city of strangers is even harder
than life on his reservation.

Many have learned the ways of the city.
Many have gone to universities. As do people
of all races, many work to pay their way
through the university. Some have scholarships
that help them through school.

As do people of all races, Indians who finish their studies at the universities choose the work they do. They have become teachers and nurses, ministers and priests, scientists, doctors, lawyers, artists. Some return to the large reservations to help their people. Many stay outside and work for the good of all Indians.

Many Indians are among the best baseball players and football players.

Many men and women of Indian or part-Indian blood have become famous.

Maria Martinez is known for the beautiful pottery she has made. Maria Tallchief and her sister Marjorie gave pleasure to those who saw their dancing. Wise and funny Will Rogers twirled a lariat while he talked. Charles Curtis was chosen by all Americans to be Vice President of the United States.

Many who live outside the reservation work on farms or ranches. Others are guides

for the hunters in the mountains. Some stay
in the city to work in filling stations. Many
Indians are steel workers. Sure-footed and
unafraid, they work on the high steel frames
of new buildings.

Many have learned new ways, but learning
in a strange place has never been easy.

Chapter XI

WHAT THE INDIAN
HAS GIVEN US

The Indian has given many things to his country.

He gave thousands of names to states and cities, mountains, rivers, and lakes. He gave the names of Massachusetts, Kansas, Chicago, Seattle, Erie, Mississippi, and many more.

To the English language he gave hundreds of new words. Wigwam, chipmunk, cactus, squash, moose, raccoon are all Indian words.

He gave other things. When the settlers

first came to America, the friendly Indian gave them friendship.

He helped them find their way over Indian trails.

The Indian gave the settlers the seeds of squash and corn, beans and tomatoes.

He showed them how to take syrup from the maple tree.

He gave new foods—corn and wild turkey, beans and potatoes, pumpkins and melons.

In friendly trade, he brought them furs.

He shared leaves and barks and roots to use for medicine.

He taught them to use canoes, hammocks, toboggans, and snowshoes.

To the children, he gave the rubber ball.

Today, books are filled with his stories.

He gave his music, and his painting, his silvermaking and his pottery, his weaving and his dance.

He has gone to war to fight for his country.

There are 600,000 Indians in America. This is a much smaller number than it was when the colonists first came, but their number is growing larger.

Whether the Indian is in Indian Country or in the city, his loyalty to his family and to his own tribe remains strong. His pride is not lessened. He wants the right to choose where he will go—whether he will go to the city, or stay on his own reservation. If he chooses to stay on his reservation, he wants this right "as long as the grass shall grow and the rivers run."

He wants to work to help himself and his family. Whether he is on the reservation, or whether he is in the city, he wants the right to be different if he chooses.

He is Indian and proud of it. He is the first American.

INDEX

antelope, hunting for, 22

baskets, 15, 41, 49, 53
beads, from shells, 12
beans, 11, 12, 13, 39, 45, 53
belts, 14-15, 48
blankets, 24, 53
bowls, from cedar trees, 24
bows and arrows, 11, 22, 24, 25
buffalo, 16, 18, 20, 27

cactus, fruit of, 15
canoes, 11, 18-19, 22
cedar trees, uses of, 24
cities, Indians in, 54-59
clothing: of woodland Indians, 10-11; buffalo for, 20; of western Indians, 21, 24; of Five Tribes, 32; of Havasupai, 38; of Navahos, 46; on reservations, 54; in Indian Centers, 55; of plains Indians, 55
clubs, 11, 24, 25
colonists, Indians and, 12, 28-29, 32, 60-61
corn, 11, 12, 13, 15, 38-39, 48, 53
council, tribal, 37, 48
Curtis, Charles, 58

dancing, 6-7, 8, 19, 42, 51, 55, 58
deer, 9, 10, 12, 22, 27
deserts, Indians of, 5, 13-15, 26, 44
drums, 19, 20
dry paintings, 52

eagle feather, 20, 55
English, speaking of, 47, 54

fishing, 9, 21, 22, 25

Five Tribes, 32
food: sharing of, 5-6, 57; deer for, 12; from cactus, 15; from buffalo, 20; from seeds, 21; for Northern Indians, 25; for reservations, 34; of Havasupai, 38-40; of Navahos, 45, 48, 53; new, from Indians, 61
forests, Indians in, 5, 22-24, 26

gifts, from Indians, 60-61
grass: for clothing, 10-11, 24; for baskets, 15, 49, 53
grasslands, Indians in, 5
Great Spirit, 7, 27
guides, Indians as, 41, 59

Havasupai, 36-42
helmets, of wood, 24
hogans, 45
houses: sharing of, 6, 57; of woodland Indians, 9-10; of desert Indians, 13, 14; of western Indians, 23; of Northern Indians, 25; of colonists, 28; of Havasupai, 37; of Navahos, 44-45, 50
hunting, 9, 11, 12, 16, 20, 22, 25, 27

illness, on reservations, 41, 46
Indian Center, 55

land, Indians and, 9, 21, 26-34, 53
language, 6, 18, 47
laws, tribal, 37, 48
longhouses, 9

maple tree, sap from, 9, 61
Martinez, Maria, 58
masks, from cedar trees, 24